This Panther Ausf.A of I./Pz.Rgt.26 was knocked out by concentrated fire from Shermans of 20th NZ Armoured Regiment at a crossroads in Palazzo Guerrino, near Sesto Imolese, Italy on 13 April 1945. It is shown being inspected by British troops on the 16th April. The vehicle has protective covers over the louvres on the rear plate and extra spaced armour on the turret roof. The Panther had disabled a Firefly and shot at a Sherman IB (105mm) before being knocked out. Previous to February 1945 I./Pz.Rgt.26 was known as I./Pz.Rgt.4. **IWM**

The power of the PIAT. These two Panther Ausf.G, tactical numbers 424 and 434, were knocked out by Corporal J.L. Tucker of 27th NZ Battalion during the night of the 15/16 April 1945 using a PIAT anti tank projector. The location is Sesto Imolese, just over the Sillaro river. The top photo shows the scene at daybreak. Of interest is the amount of foliage carried by both vehicles; testament to Allied air superiority. The photo below shows the scene a little later on. NZ troops have turned the turret of tank 424 ready for removal and 434's has been turned to clear the road.

2x J.Plowman

A rear view clearly shows the protective covers installed over the air intake and exhaust louvres on the engine deck. The modifications were made by the I-Staffel or maintenance units probably during January or February 1945. I./Pz.Rgt.26 used small tactical numbers on the turret sides and rear as can be seen here. These vehicles were part of the last shipment from Germany.

J.Plowman

Tank 424 awaits it's fate, meanwhile interested New Zealand soldiers look over the beast and pose for photos. Both tank 424 and 434 were from the October production batch which accounts for the lack of Zimmerit and the addition of the raised fan for the Kampfraumheizung or crew compartment heater on the rear deck, this does not appear to have a protective cover.

ATL

The covers on the engine deck were made from pieces of 5mm thick Schürzen and were a Waffenamt authorised field modification from December 1944 to increase protection from artillery splinters and strafing aircraft. The crew have gone to some effort to camouflage their vehicle with large swathes of foliage on the rear clearing the exhausts and foliage over chicken wire on the turret.

ATL

New Zealanders pose for the ubiquitous trophy photo with tank 434 in it's final resting place - a drainage ditch. The camouflage materials can be clearly seen on the glacis plate and on the gun. The vehicle appears to have lost one or two of the outer roadwheels.
ATL

April 17 1945. A Panther of I./Pz.Rgt.26 has ended up in a bomb crater in Medicina courtesy of D.A.F. - Desert Air Force. The supplemental spaced armour on the turret roof was constructed in a sandwich, which can be seen in this shot, as can the camouflage pattern on the gun barrel. In the background is a Wasp flamethrower going at full pelt.

ATL

7

A view from the other side shows the surrounding destruction especially to the railway cars in the background. Unlike the vehicles seen on the previous pages no tactical numbers are to be seen on the sides or rear of the turret. The inset photo shows another unfortunate Panther Ausf.G turned turtle in a roadside ditch in the Medicina area.

1x ATL, 1x MNP

This poorly exposed shot taken by a serviceman shows tracks and ammunition for the 7.5cm Kw.K.42 strewn around the crater. The New Zealand soldier is standing with a Sprgr.42 high explosive round. Just visible in the background is a Bergepanther Ausf.A recovery vehicle captured intact.

J.Plowman

Another crater, another Panther of I./Pz.Rgt.26, this time in the area of Massa Lombarda, April 1945. The open engine hatch shows the details of the engine with one of the square air filters is missing. The vehicle carries extra foliage for camouflage plus extra mud and dirt with the help of the Desert Air Force.
J.Plowman

A few days later and the vehicle is still attracting attention, this time from Polish troops. Parts of the engine deck have been "liberated" revealing the radiators and fan. The lack of foliage shows the shape of the spaced armour with cut outs for the lifting hooks at the front and Nahverteidigungswaffe at the rear of the turret roof. **MNP**

The carcass of an Elefant of 1.Kp/s.Pz.Jg.Abt.653 on a roadside in Italy sometime around June 1944. This behemoth has been cannibalized by the maintenance platoon as is evident from the lack of running gear and propped up front end. Just visible under the fenders are the rounded track guides used on the Elefant - a detail not often seen. Scoops from incoming armour piercing rounds have scarred the nose of the vehicle, another has hit the left hand final drive and this is most likely what disabled the vehicle.

L.Archer

A 75mm shot into the 30mm side armour above the second bogie has brewed this Panzer IV/70(V) of s.H.Pz.Jg.Abt.655, dislodging the roof in the process. It was photographed by Canadian Army photographers at a crossroads east of Materborn, near Kleve, Germany in February 1945 where s.H.Pz.Jg.Abt.655 had been supporting the 84 Infanterie Division. Armed with the powerful 7.5cm PaK42 L/70 gun, 80mm frontal armour and a low silhouette, these vehicles were a formidable opponent, but like all vehicles without a turret they were vulnerable when attacked from the sides or rear. **2x PAC**

GIs of the 301st Infantry Regiment, 94 Infantry Division pose for a snapshot alongside a late production Pz.Kpfw.IV Ausf.J in the Hunsrück Mountains, west of the Rhine, during January or February 1945. The tank belonged to II./Pz.Rgt.15, 11 Panzer Division, the black painted tactical number being typical of this unit. An emblem is barely visible on the turret front. Like many photos of the period it has been transformed into a Tiger tank by the photographer. **L.Archer**

Left: US combat medics look over the wreck of a late Pz.Kpfw.IV Ausf.J in the Ruhr pocket in April 1945, although they stand little chance of reviving this patient. The late war modifications are quite evident: pivoting cupola lid, deleted gunner's vision port, wire mesh side skirts and simplified towing points. A rare and unusual sight is the poison gas detector panel fitted to it's mounting on top of the gun. In the presence of poison gas this would have turned a wine red colour.　　**2x L.Archer**

Above: A barely discernible camouflage pattern can be seen on the cupola of this Pz.Kpfw.III Ausf.N, the sides of the turret have been left in plain Dunkelgelb as they would have been covered by Schürzen, part of which is missing here. No date or location are available.　　**L.Archer**

A pair of Steyr built Schienenpanzerspähwagen snapped by a US serviceman at the war's end. These were armed with a 7.5cm Kw.K L/24 in the turret of a Pz.Kpfw.III Ausf.N plus gun ports on all sides. From November 1944 a schwere Schienenpanzerspähzug would have had two of these cars, two radio cars, four infantry cars, two flak cars with 2cm FlaKvierling or 3.7cm FlaK and two armoured flatcars for Pz.Kpfw.38(t). The domed objects on the front and side are air inlets for the Steyr 3.5 litre V8 diesel engine.

L.Archer

This holed Pz.Kpfw.IV Ausf.J of 6.Kp/SS Pz.Rgt.2 lost an encounter with 117th Infantry Regiment, 30th US Infantry Division on the outskirts of St Fromond, France during July 1944 and is about to be hauled away by an M1A1 heavy wrecker. In addition to the penetrations in the armour it is interesting to note the effect of small arms fire on the Zimmerit coating on the turret front. **US Army**

A GI's snapshot taken in a battered garage of Stab Pz.Ers u Ausb.Abt.35 at Bamberg, Germany during April 1945. Amidst the rubble is this September 1942 vintage Pz.Kpfw.IV Ausf.G and in the background a Pz.Kpfw.III. The engine in the foreground is an incomplete Maybach HL230 P30 as used in the Panther tank. The sign on the wall behind reads: "Rauchen verboten" - smoking prohibited.   **L.Archer**

If it doesn't work, dig it in. A reworked Pz.Kpfw.III Ausf.E or F of Pz.Ers u Ausb.Abt.35 in a hull down position defending the garages shown on the previous page. The vehicles were organised into Panzerkampfgruppe von Hobbe and later von Massenbach. Careful inspection of the vehicles in front of the garages shows various marks of Pz.Kpfw.I and II.

L.Archer

19

Stripped bare. Whether by German maintenance units or local Italians they have made a thorough job of it. This Panther Ausf.A number 215 of I./Pz.Rgt.4 was lost in the vicinity of Rimini during September 1944, although it is likely that this photo taken by New Zealand soldiers was taken some time later. The large hole in the engine compartment floor is the engine oil drain.

J.Plowman

A Panzerbeobachtungswagen III - armoured artillery observation vehicle, based on a Pz.Kpfw.III Ausf.G found abandoned by Canadian forces in Trun, France, August 1944. The cupola has remains of the original Dunkelgrau colour showing as stripes indicating that the vehicle was painted with the cupola observation slits closed.

The vehicle belonged to either 1.SS, 9.SS or 12.SS Panzer Division. The upper inset photo shows the TSR-1 observation periscope in use by a curious Canadian soldier.

3x PAC

An abandoned but complete looking Sd.Kfz.138/1 Ausf.M Grille photographed somewhere in Normandy 1944. Apart from some dead looking foliage it has received no other camouflage on it's Dunkelgelb paintwork. A possible penetration in the rear side armour and a dent in the gun are the only signs of damage. It looks like Allied troops have been over the vehicle looking for mementos as there are opened boxes and papers strewn about. The chassis number, 3283, is stencilled to the side of the driver's visor.

I.Kinnear

A Bergepanther Ausf.G of 19 Panzer Division has become mired in a muddy hole and abandoned by it's crew in the face of the 1st Czechoslovak Independent Tank Brigade near Bolatice, Czechoslovakia, 1945. DEMAG began production of the Ausf.G vehicles in October 1944. Armament consisted of an MG34 in a ball mount and a mount for an AA MG welded to the radio operator's periscope guard.
2x VHA

An immense explosion has ripped the front from the this late Pz.Kpfw.IV Ausf.J, peeling back the side wall and blowing the turret roof upside down. It lacks the gunner's vision port, but has the old model hull with bolted on towing points. The car in the picture below is a Skoda Superb 3000

About as rare a tank as you will find. An extremely poor, but invaluable, image of the only Panther II hull completed by M.A.N. as it was found by US forces. The vehicle is today preserved at the Patton Museum in Kentucky USA with an April 1945 vintage Ausf.G turret, which we can now see was fitted after the war. The structure in its place has an opened hatch on top. Unfortunately no date or location are given.
W.Auerbach

The back of this veteran's photo reads: "This was taken in the Cerise forest. That's Jim Cosgrove and Russ Adams in the picture. We had a collection point there for a while for captured equipment - some we repaired and others were just kept for parts. The tank or gun carrier on the right was booby trapped". The location is actually Cerisy la Foret; a village outside Bayeux, France. Of interest is the difference between the Balkenkreuz on the sides of the two Sturmgeschütze.

L.Archer

In the process of rebuilding a Sturmgeschütz III Ausf.G are Tec. 3 Victor Eicher and Tec. 4 E.W. Thacker of 528 Heavy Maintenance Company. Chef-du-Pont, France 11 August 1944. It appears that the final drive has been removed from the vehicle on the left to be fitted to this one. Note that the donor vehicle on the left is missing many of the bolts from the driver's front plate.

US Army

US officers and a German officer, possibly General Lucht discuss the finer points of a Tiger II of s.H.Pz.Abt.507 in Osterode, Germany, 24 April 1945. The backdrop is the Hotel Kaiserhof, the command post of the US 8th Armoured Division between 23 and 25 April. The massive vehicle had been knocked out by a 90mm round into the turret side and was moved into the Dörgestrasse by the maintenance unit of s.H.Pz.Abt.507 where it was photographed on 12 April by US Army photographers. It was subsequently moved outside the Hotel Kaiserhof clearing the narrow Dörgestrasse.

2x US Army

One of the last Tiger IIs produced by Henschel during March 1945 and collected by 3.Kp/s.H.Pz.Abt.511. This vehicle has ribbed mudguards and 18 tooth drive sprockets driving the 660mm wide Verladkette (transport track). The 18 tooth drive sprockets were for use with a new single link cross country track which this vehicle did not receive. Like many wrecks it has been pushed off the road, bending the track guards in the process.

J.Scott

Three views of Jagdtiger 323 of 3.Kp/s.Pz.Jg.Abt.653 abandoned in Neustadt am der Weinstrasse, Germany on 23 March 1945. It had been part of the three Jagdtiger strong Kampfgruppe Göggerle (numbers 323, 331 and 234), commanded by Lt. Kaspar Göggerle in Jagdtiger 331. Vehicle 323 had broken down while backing into a garden on Landauer Strasse and was abandoned. Over the street vehicle 331 carried on firing until the crew drained the recoil cylinder on the last round, rendering it useless to the Americans. Vehicle 331 is now at Aberdeen Proving Ground in the USA.

2x W.Auerbach, 1x C.Ankerstjerne

These views of the front of Jagdtiger 323 show why it was such a formidable weapon. Numerous hits from Shermans and M10s of US 10th Armoured Division have bounced off the thick frontal armour, much to the American crews horror.

Like the other photos it is shown after being towed to the Festival Platz from it's original position in the garden by French occupation troops. The three Jagdtigers of Kampfgruppe Göggerle accounted for 25 US tanks destroyed.   **2x W.Auerbach**

The sections of spare track carried on the superstructure side are unusual in that normally a bridge link and connecting link were carried on each hook. Here we have a bit of everything. Note the scars on the gun mantlet and on the lower nose plate. The tactical number has been painted in red or black and on page 30 the paint runs are visible.

W.Auerbach

If only these children knew what destruction this 75 ton monster had caused. It stayed at the Festival Platz until 1948 when it was scrapped, a fate that befell the majority of the vehicles in this book. By now it is missing it's gun travel lock, but has gained some towing cables and a steel bar across the towing eyes at the front. **W.Auerbach**

Curious GIs climb over the carcass of a Jagdtiger from 2.Kp/s.Pz.Jg.Abt.653 at a railway crossing in Zeiskam, Germany. It had been part of Kampfgruppe Göggerle, but this was the one that got away. It was disabled with a shot into the front of the right track by US tanks, after which it was blown up by the crew. The massive vehicle has sunk due to the effect of heat on it's torsion bar suspension. It is interesting to note the apparent lack of camouflage paint and tactical numbers compared to the previous photos.

L.Archer

A victim of Allied air superiority over France. A Tiger I of s.H.Pz.Abt.503 or s.SS Pz.Abt.102 destroyed in Bernay on 24 August 1944. An internal explosion has unseated the hull roof and made rather a mess of the stowage bin on the turret rear. This would account for the extensive scorching to the Zimmerit on the vehicle. There is no damage to the building or fence in the background indicating that it was probably towed here.

I.Kinnear

One of 21 Panzer Division's 24 Lg.s.FH.13(Sfl.) auf Lorraine Schlepper looking a little the worse for wear. The sides and rear of the fighting compartment have been completely blown away along with a large part of the running gear. The crew had covered the gun barrel with chicken wire to attach camouflage materials. The 21 Panzer Division lost all but one of it's Lg.s.FH.13(Sfl.) auf Lorraine Schleppers during the Normandy campaign.

US Army

2.Kp/s.H.Pz.Jg.Abt.525 lost this Nashorn in the Gothic Line area of Italy 1944. A catastrophic explosion has blown off part of the superstructure, the armour over the driver's and engine compartments and much of the running gear. With the side armour gone it is possible to see how far the gun recoiled into the fighting compartment, as the recoil cylinder was drained before firing it's last round. This rendered the weapon useless. In the background the trackless wreck of an Allied Sherman pays testament to the ferocity of the fighting.

J.Plowman

GIs inspect a diminutive 4.7cm Pak(t) auf Pz.Kpfw.35R(f) formerly owned by 3.Kp/ 517 Schnelle Abt of Schnelle Brigade 30 near Le Molay Littry, between Bayeux and St Lo, France. The date is mid June 1944. Another well known view of this vehicle can be found in Panzers in Normandy Then and Now. There was a definite advantage to being short when crewing this vehicle.

L.Archer

A Sturmgeschütz III Ausf.G from an unknown unit pushed off the side of the road near Avranches, France, 1944 by US forces. The vehicle has the MIAG pattern Zimmerit (small squares) rather than the Alkett waffle pattern. It has been left in the Dunkelgelb base paint, the only camouflage is from rust and oil stains.   **L.Archer**

This rather tired looking Marder III was photographed by a New Zealand soldier at the end of 1944 in Faenza, Italy and either belonged to 1.Kp/Pz.Jg.Abt.305, 305 Infanterie Division or 2.Kp/Pz.Jg.Abt.715, 715 Infanterie Division. It is a late production example with the welded driver's armoured hood, modified towing hooks and welded air intake. The vehicle was probably booby trapped as it has "MINES" chalked onto the side along with a barely discernible Balkenkreuz. **J.Plowman**

Another Marder III this time pushed off of the road. It is an early production vehicle as is evident from the exit of the exhaust and driver's armoured hood. A projectile has made a bit of a mess of the engine air inlet and outlet, unseating the gun in the process. The side armour was only 10mm, enough to keep the rain out. The MG34 has been fitted for AA use.

US Army

41

With a total of 32 kills rings on the barrel, a Marder III of 1.Kp/ Pz.Jg.Abt.346, 346 Infanterie Division awaits it's fate at a weapons collection dump in Utrecht, Netherlands, July 1945. It is a late production vehicle with welded air intakes has been camouflaged with a rather fetching leopard spot pattern. Additional camouflage materials would have been held by the wires that criss cross the sides. Some of the other vehicles pictured include a captured Sherman Firefly VC, Volkswagen Kübelwagen and Italian Fiat/SPA CL39 light truck.

PAC

The significance of the small white cross on the nose plate is unknown although other, possibly earlier, photographs show this vehicle with a bird and the name "Sofi" chalked onto the front. Though the vehicle had 32 kills to it's credit it would appear that something got it's own back as an armour patch has been welded to the front of the fighting compartment. Next to the Marder is a captured Firefly VC.
PAC

The Firefly was probably used by Pz.Kp.224. No Allied insignia can be seen apart from the small triangle stencilled on the left of the rear plate indicating that it once belonged to "A" squadron. According to a Canadian Army report the vehicle still had it's name "Aventure" although that cannot be seen here. The long stowage box on the rear plate was a standard fitting of the Firefly and contained various tools, covers and most importantly 4 greatcoats. **PAC**

The business end of "Aventure" shows an unusual surprise; a muzzle brake from a German 7.5cm gun. The glacis plate has been liberally clad in spare track to give a little extra protection. A Balkenkreuz is just visible on the turret side. **PAC**

In the same dump at Utrecht was this turretless Pz.Kpfw.II Ausf A, B or C. It would have been used as a gun tractor or munitions carrier for the Panzerjäger unit. The large triangular aerial trough on the fender has been removed - although the aerial remains. A three colour camouflage pattern has been sprayed in wavy lines. The vehicle to the left is an armoured Sd.Kfz.7/1 or 7/2.

PAC

The turret ring was covered by a wooden plate with a square hole in the middle and covered in light gauge sheet steel. The camouflage pattern can be clearly seen on the side of the superstructure. **2x PAC**

Old tanks never die. These veteran Pz.Kpfw.IIs from the early campaigns were ready to soldier on as munitions vehicles, until the US 6th Armoured Division captured them at Mühlhausen, Germany 10 April 1945. Various versions of Munitionspanzer II can be seen on the train.

US Army

This is the third vehicle from the back carrying the number 226 on the superstructure and what would appear to be the tactical sign for the second Kompanie of a Panzer Regiment. Unlike the vehicle shown at Utrecht these examples have no cover over the turret ring.

US Army

Private J.R. Wise of US 68th Tank Battalion takes a closer look at this Munitionspanzer II based on an Ausf.b chassis. The first leaf spring has sprung round leaving the second roadwheel up against the return roller and an armour patch has been welded onto an old war wound on the middle of the 13mm thick rounded nose plate. All of the Munitionspanzers on the train were painted in plain, weathered Dunkelgelb with no camouflage pattern. **US Army**

A captured M3 light tank destroyed by Russian forces on Saaremaa Island, Estonia, 1944. The original cupola mounted MG has been retained. Of particular interest are the two slightly different Balkenkreuz painted in white on the hull side. The diminutive size of the M3 is quite obvious next to the soldier.

EFA

A GI inspects Buffalo Bill, a captured American M8 armoured car, known as a Panzerspähwagen M8(a), East of St Vith, Belgium on 3 February 1945. This vehicle has been left in the original olive drab colour with some very hastily applied Balkenkreuz - the one on the rear of the turret having no white outline. The original caption claims that it was knocked out by US artillery.

US Army

Useful antiques. A Pz.Kpfw.17/18 R 730(f) earns its keep for the US Army as a tractor after being captured from German forces. It has a Balkenkreuz painted on the side and nose over Dunkelgrau paintwork. The armament has been removed and a plate with a hole in it welded over the aperture, also a section of the cupola has been removed or more likely broken off. The two photos on the right show a Luftwaffe operated vehicle painted in Dunkelgelb. The small size of the FT17 is obvious in comparison to the GI.

3x L.Archer

Two GIs pose for a snapshot with the trackless wreck of a munitions carrier or artillery tractor on the chassis of the Pz.Kpfw.35 R 731(f). Our man on the right is brandishing a German stick grenade. A black circular unit symbol is just visible on the left fender. No location or date are given. **L.Archer**

A snapshot of a Flakpanzer 38(t) abandoned in Normandy, probably by SS.Pz.Rgt.12, 12.SS Panzer Division. The vehicle and other wreckage has been roped off and a danger sign hung on the fender. The camouflage pattern has been applied by waving a spray gun and additional foliage has been put on the vehicle - note how the camouflage pattern has been applied to the inside of the hinged superstructure armour plates.
L.Archer

Another somewhat dishevelled example of a Flakpanzer 38(t) in a muddy vehicle dump in Normandy. The single 2cm Flak 38 lacked the required firepower to deal with low flying ground attack aircraft and as such the Flakpanzer 38(t) got the raw end of the deal. None of the 84 vehicles that fought in Normandy survived. This one has lost a number of the hinged superstructure armour plates

US Army

A rare sight. A production Flakpanzer Ostwind photographed in Nové Benátky, northeast of Prague in May 1945. Ostwinds were to be built on new chassis with modified superstructures: a Tiger I turret ring, relocated radio operator's hatch and "U" shaped lugs now appeared on the top corners of the front plate. The 3.7cm FlaK43/1, seen at full elevation, is missing its muzzle brake.

VHA

Two very poor quality but rare photographs taken in France by a US serviceman of a late production Flakpanzer IV Möbelwagen with the 25mm plate platform sides. Torsion bars incorporated into the sides made raising and lowering them an easy task It is unclear how the vehicle met it's end but the gun barrel is missing. The inset picture shows the details of the 3.7cm FlaK43.

2x W.Auerbach

"Hedi", a Flakpanzer IV Möbelwagen from the Pz.Fla-Zug of St.Kp/s.Pz.Jg.Abt.654 is being inspected by British soldiers at a weapons collection point. The Balkenkreuz on the driver's front plate is peculiar to s.Pz.Jg.Abt.654.

PAC

A GI poses with "Gudrun"; a Sturmpanzer 43 of St.Pz.Abt.217 in Elbeuf, France September 1945. Having escaped the carnage of the Falaise pocket in August 1944 her fate was destruction by her crew. Of interest are the insignia on the gun above the name and the dark colour of the Zimmerit.

L.Archer

A US Army bulldozer gets to grips with the 28 ton wreck of a Sturmpanzer 43 of St.Pz.Abt.216 in the Lazio region of Italy sometime during June 1944. The vehicle has been penetrated below the driver's visor blowing off one of the steering brake hatches and the transmission access panel. The loader's hatch has gone and part of the superstructure roof has been displaced by the explosion. It is an early production vehicle based on the chassis of the Pz.Kpfw.IV Ausf G. **US Army**

Men of the 309th Medical Battalion, 84th Division check a Sd.Kfz.250/7 mortar carrier of 9 Panzer Division for booby traps near Geilenkirchen, Germany, 16 December 1944. It will eventually be converted into an ambulance. The vehicle has a crack in the armour on the rear corner of the superstructure. The rack on the rear wall carried spools of telephone cable. Note the amount of dirt thrown up by the fenderless front wheel. **US Army**

GIs look over the burning wreck of a Sd.Kfz.250.nA of 2 Panzer Division that was ambushed by the 213th Tank Destroyer Battalion near St. Aubin D'Appetat, France on 14 August 1944. This vehicle and others had been retreating from a trap. The door has been blown off of the storage box between the tracks and front wheel exposing the drawers.
US Army

Another Sd.Kfz.250.nA, this time near Elva, Estonia after being ambushed by Russian forces. Note the scorching around the front visors and plain Dunkelgelb paintwork. Local inhabitants most likely removed the front wheels if they were intact. Lurking in the treeline is a burnt out Panther. **EFA**

Further along the road lie these two shattered Sd.Kfz.251 Ausf.D. The lead vehicle has lost it's armoured rear section, the right armoured wall landing by the side of the vehicle and penetrations can be seen in the side of the engine compartment.

Although difficult to tell it is looks as if it has been fitted with the later cast tracks. Behind is a Sd.Kfz.251/17 with a 2cm gun in Schwebelafette swivelling mount.

EFA

A look at the carnage from the rear shows the thoroughly burnt out Sd.Kfz.251/17. Russian soldiers are busy inspecting the damage inflicted to the Sd.Kfz.251 in the previous photo. A third halftrack can be seen at the head of the convoy.

EFA

A far cry from the usual horse drawn carts is this Sd.Kfz.251 Ausf.D which makes a most unusual mode of transport for a family of Romanian refugees. They are pictured at a camp in Wallern, Czechoslovakia on 18 June 1945. A rudimentary roof has been fabricated in the same way as the carts visible in the background and a German Zeltbahn waterproof shelter triangle covers the back of the roof. The rain guards over the stowage boxes on the panniers are a late war addition.

US Army

The front end of a Sd.Kfz.251/7 rearranged courtesy of the US 26th Division and photographed in Eschdorf, Luxembourg on 29 December 1944. It presents us an unusual view of the engine compartment. In the background a GI is looking over a knocked out Panther, the torsion bar suspension having sagged as a result of fire. Both previously belonged to the Führer Grenadier Brigade.

US Army

Looking like it was painted in the 1970s is this 2cm FlaK38 auf Sf Zkgw.3t with a striking hand painted camouflage pattern. An explosion behind the driver has distorted the top and side plates of the armoured front. Of interest is the unit emblem of an eagle on a cannon that has been painted onto the nose. Like many disabled vehicles it is missing the front wheels.

L.Archer

A bent and battered example of a Sd.Kfz.7 artillery tractor found on a train in Czechoslovakia during 1945 and photographed by a soldier of the US 704th Tank Destroyer Battalion. The paintwork appears rather dark to be the standard Dunkelgelb and is more likely Dunkelgrau. One of the fenders, with width indicator, has ended up under the rail wagon.

L.Archer

What appears at first glance to be a Sd.Kfz.7 is actually an Italian built Breda 61 towing a 15cm sFH 404(i) photographed in the Bologna area during April 1945. The Breda 61 differed from the German Sd.Kfz.7 by being right hand drive and having a longer bonnet; both of which can be seen in the photo. A rather dashing "wave the spray gun" camouflage pattern has been applied by the crew.

L.Archer

Fire has ravaged a Sd.Kfz.8 DB10 prime mover photographed by a US soldier near Bologna, Italy in 1945. All that is left of the tyres on the roadwheels is white ash.

The DB10 was the final version of the 12 ton prime mover and was produced by Daimler-Benz, Krauss-Maffei, ELMAG and Skoda. **L.Archer**

A closer look at the front mudguard reveals the 334 Infanterie Division unit insignia. The camouflage pattern is discernible among the scorch marks on the mudguards and radiator. The two cans with pipes in the engine compartment are air filters for the Maybach HL85 TURKM V12 engine.

L.Archer

Looking more like a tea bag than a tracked carrier, is this RSO/01 which has been well and truly shot up, but has not burnt out. The image is a still from a film made by the US 163rd Signal Photo Company in Italy, May 1944 with the British 8th Army.

US Army

This RSO/01 from an SS unit was hitched to a 7.5cm PaK40 just off a road junction before being destroyed. The barrel of the gun is lying to the left of the picture - out of frame. The back of the cab is peppered with shell fragment holes and the driver's door has a large hole in it. The unit and the location are not known, although another picture of this vehicle has the notation "through France" on it.

L.Archer

A Sd.Kfz.223 Ausf.B and Sd.Kfz.233 photographed on a railway flatcar in Italy by a US serviceman, probably in 1943. The Sd.Kfz.250 alte Art on the far right could be a Funkpanzerwagen (Sd.Kfz.250/3) or a Beobachtungswagen (Sd.Kfz.250/4 or 5) as it has an aerial mount on the left rear of the body.

L.Archer

17.SS Panzergrenadier Division lost this Sd.Kfz.223 Ausf.B at Isigny, France to US artillery. The rear of the vehicle and turret show evidence of a fierce fire, burning away two of the four aerial supports and the rear tyre. A tactical sign is visible on the nearest mudguard. An outline of the shovel can be seen on the vehicle - someone forgot to remove it before spraying the camouflage pattern. The two triangular objects on the front fenders are the opened lids of fender stowage boxes.

US Army

Polish soldiers look over a Sturmgeschütz M43 mit 105/25 853(i) from 278 or 305 Infanterie Division near Medicina, Italy. It was knocked out by Pulk 4 Pancerny Skorpion (4th Polish Armoured Regiment "Scorpion") or 14/20th King's Hussars Regiment around 16 April 1945. The low height of the vehicle is obvious. **MNP**

One way of getting apples from a tree. This Sturmgeschütz III Ausf.G has a good tally of kills, but the killing days are over. Chunks of Zimmerit have been shot away, as has the driver's Fahrersehklappe 50 visor, the top of the commander's cupola and part of the muzzle brake. It was photographed in Holland, 19 September 1944.

US Army

One rare cat. A Panther Ausf.G abandoned between Opava and Ostrava, Czechoslovakia at the end of the war. It was one of only 28 vehicles assembled by M.A.N. during March/April 1945 and is easily identified by the steel wheel on the last roadwheel station. The turret side has rings for attaching camouflage introduced during March 1945 and the faint outlined tactical number 543. The inset photo was taken later allowing time for the wheels to be spirited away. The vehicle belonged to 8, 17 or 19 Panzer Division.

1x M.Solar, 1x VHA

Another of M.A.N.'s last Panthers. It has all the features expected of a Panther at this late stage of the war such as: new anti aircraft MG mount on the cupola, turret camouflage rings, chin on the mantlet, steel wheel on the last wheel station, larger self cleaning idler and Flammenvernichter - flame suppressing exhausts. The rear plate does not have mountings for infra red equipment sometimes seen on Panthers produced at this time.

W.Auerbach

The 80mm front plate of this unknown Jagdpanther with it's battle scars tells a story of the bravery of Allied tank crews. The scar on the joint of the front plates has split the interlocking weld and possibly damaged the gearbox - at the very least someone inside would have a nasty headache.
C.Ankerstjerne

A Jagdpanther of an unknown unit lies burnt out in a field. Fire has lowered the suspension and turned the tyres to ash. The vehicle was assembled after December 1944 as is it has the single driver's periscope opening, raised fan tower on the engine deck and revised external stowage. One cowl of the Flammenvernichter exhausts can just be seen behind this. It is difficult to determine if there is a camouflage pattern on the vehicle or if it is the effects of fire.

L.Archer

A very unusual sight; a Panther Ausf.A retrofitted with Flammenvernichter exhausts, most likely from I./Pz.Rgt.15, 11 Panzer Division. The beast was photographed by PFC. Eino. J. Mackie of US 274th Infantry Regiment, 70th Infantry Division near Bad Hersfeld, Germany, April 1945. It is also notable for the relocated cleaning rod tube on the rear deck, spare roadwheel on the turret and slab of missing armour plate on the hull side. In the foreground are a couple of unused Panzerfaust warheads.

E.Mackie

A partially whitewashed Befehls-Panther Ausf.G of II./Pz.Rgt.33, 9 Panzer Division gets a once over by a GI of the 6th Armoured Division in Wilwerdange, Luxembourg 25 January 1945. Extra radios in these vehicles meant room had to be found so the co-axial MG was omitted and the hole in the mantlet plugged as seen here. Note the large armoured aerial base on the rear deck between the exhausts.

US Army

A sorry looking Panzer IV/70(A) belonging to 7.Kp/Pz.Rgt.2, Panzer Brigade 103 destroyed near Mühlhausen in December 1944 during the fighting in the Alsace. At this time 7.Kp/Pz.Rgt.2 was attached to Panzer Brigade 106. Hooks for hanging extra tracks on the driver's plate are visible on the superstructure front. **K.Münch**

T/Sgt. Luther. W. Johnson of US 36th Infantry Division poses with another Panzer IV/70(A) of 7.Kp/Pz.Rgt.2 that was attached to Panzer Brigade 106. As seen on the previous page, extra track has been fitted to the driver's front plate, the nose and to the side of the fighting compartment above the wire mesh Schürzen. This is a later production vehicle with towing eyes formed from the lower hull sides.

L.Archer

Yet another Panzer IV/70(A) of 7.Kp/Pz.Rgt.2 attached to Panzer Brigade 106, here photographed by the US 1st Infantry Division at Himberg, Germany on 19 March 1945. It would appear that vehicles issued to 7.Kp/Pz.Rgt.2 had stayed with the Brigade since their employment in the Alsace in December 1944. This example has a battle scar on the mantlet and evidence of an internal explosion which has lifted the roof of the fighting compartment.

US Army

These vehicles from 5.Kp./Pz.Abt. Führer Begleit Brigade were knocked out in Chenogne, near Bastogne during the Ardennes offensive. The example in the foreground has been holed through the side of the fighting compartment. Careful study of the lower photo shows a third vehicle lurking to the right.

2x S.De Meyer

A Panzer IV/70(A) of either H.Stu.Art.Brig.280 or 667 knocked out during a counter attack on Volxsheim, Germany, 18 March 1945 in an attempt to halt the advance of US XII Corps. These photos are clear proof that the Vorsatz P mounting actually saw service. The Vorsatz P was a 90° curved barrel in a ball mount fitted into the loader's hatch. This permitted the use of an MP44 to provide close in protection to the blindspots of the vehicle, vision being by WZF 5811 periscope. The entire left side of the superstructure has been blown away along with much of the running gear.

C.Ellis

The Vorsatz P mount is much clearer in this front view. Unlike many of the other examples of Panzer IV/70(A) shown here this has no extra track on the driver's front plate, only on the nose. The slab of armour plate next to the gun is the rotating cover for the loader's MG42. The contents of the fighting compartment have been blown out of the side of the vehicle and are lying on the ground.

C.Ellis

A Czech soldier climbs over a Panzer IV/70(A) of 6.Kp/Pz.Rgt.39, 17 Panzer Division, knocked out by two shots from a T-34/85 in Koberice, Czechoslovakia, 15 April 1945. The shots penetrated the right side killing the crew. Many Panzer IV/70(A) had the Balkenkreuz painted very close to the top of the superstructure on the front and sides, this vehicle is no exception. Note the broken track on the far side of the vehicle.

2x VHA

This Panzer IV/70(A) originally belonged to 24 Panzer Division until January 1945 when it was handed over to 23 Panzer Division. It is pictured here as a casualty of Unternehmen Fruhlingserwachen - Operation Spring Awakening near Hejmakser, Hungary in March 1945. The vehicle has been short tracked, running the tracks around the remaining wheels so it can be towed, by Russian forces ready for rail shipment to Russia. Note the two types of towing points on the front plate and the Vorsatz P mounting in the loader's hatch. The Panther in the background is from either 23 Panzer Division or 1.SS Panzer Division.

M.Bayerl

A late production Hummel captured by the US 8th Infantry Division in the area of Schwerin, Germany and photographed on 11 May 1945. The vehicle could have belonged to 25 Panzer Grenadier Division or more likely 7 Panzer Division. The chassis number has been stencilled onto the left of the nose plate over the top of the hand painted camouflage.

Captain Hans L. Trefousse, an interrogation officer with the 69th Infantry Division poses atop the late production Hummel he captured single handed by talking the crew into following him back through the lines near Wurzen, Germany, 25 April 1945. The name "Heidi" and the number 6 have been painted on the superstructure side, behind this is a faint Balkenkreuz. Part of the chassis number is visible on the front plate as a small black 753.

US Army

Once the pride of the Panzerwaffe, now junk. At least that what it says on the side. This Pz.Kpfw.IV Ausf.H of II./Pz.Rgt.16, 116 Panzer Division was knocked out near the castle of Bourg St Leonard, France during August 1944. An explosion inside the tank has blown off the driver's and radio operator's hatches. The horseshoe on the turret skirt seems to have brought this crew little luck.

I.Kinnear

Two views of what are possibly the same Sturmgeschütz III Ausf.E taken by two different US servicemen. This old veteran has been left in the Dunkelgelb base paint with no camouflage pattern added. A good proportion of the fenders have been bent or are missing - a sign of hard combat perhaps? A total of 284 Ausf.E were completed before production switched to the Ausf.F with the longer StuK 40 gun in March 1942. Note the specifications written on the fighting compartment side where the gun cleaning rods would normally be carried.

2x L.Archer

Once the chariots of 3.Kp/SS.Pz.Rgt.12, these Panthers were destroyed on the morning of 9 June 1944 along the railway line between Norrey en Bessin and Bretteville l'Orgueilleuse, France by nine Sherman Fireflies of the Canadian Elgin Regiment. Of the twelve Panthers committed, seven were lost on the battlefield, six to the 17pdr guns of the Fireflies and one to a PIAT of the Canadian Regina Rifles. Some of these were later put to use as training targets, which explains their sorry state.

5x L.Archer